THE
TAO OF YODA

Other Books by D. W. Kreger:

The Secret Tao: Uncovering the Hidden History and Meaning of Lao Tzu. With a revised translation of the Tao Te Ching.

2012 & The Mayan Prophecy of Doom: The Definitive Guide to Mythology and Science Behind the 2012 Prophecies.

THE
TAO OF YODA

BASED UPON THE TAO TE CHING, BY LAO TZU

INTRODUCTION AND TRANSLATION BY
D. W. KREGER

WINDHAM EVERITT

First Edition 2013

Cataloging-in-Publication-Data-on-file

ISBN: 978-0-9833099-2-5

Published by
Windham Everitt Publishing
P. O. Box 900922, Palmdale, CA 93543

Digital Distribution through
William Baughman Publishing

Printed in the United States of America

10 9 8 7 6 5 4 3 2 1

For Wolfie.
May the Force be with you always.

INTRODUCTION

Historians, philosophers, and professors of ancient literature may tell you that the philosopher named Lao Tzu, who lived in China 25 centuries ago, wrote the following passages. What they do not tell you, because they do not know, is that there is a mysterious connection between this ancient work and the modern day mythology of Star Wars.

According to history, Lao Tzu was a philosopher and a teacher of the famous Chinese philosopher Confucius. And, according to legend, it was Lao Tzu who produced the two books, one named Tao, and one named Te. Together they are known as the Tao Te Ching. But no one knows for sure that Lao Tzu was the author, or even who Lao Tzu was for certain. By the beginning of the second century BC, the books were already centuries old, and quite famous in China. Later a religion was created in China based upon this mysterious philosophy, and it was called Taoism. Modern day scholars still debate the origin these books. All we know for certain is that they are among the oldest known books on Earth.

Though the history of these passages is mysterious, one truth is obvious. Many have noticed that the philosophy of Lao Tzu appears echoed in the modern day fable of Star Wars, and specifically the wisdom of Jedi Master Yoda. But, what many do not realize is that even the way in which Lao Tzu's lines are written in Chinese is similar to Yoda's unique style of speech. This was actually a surprising and recent discovery. For many years this fact had been obscured by the existing English translations available, though there had been over 70 English translations published. The problem is that the Chinese of 2600 years ago is very different than any known Chinese dialect today, and therefore it is very difficult to translate. Then, with the most recent transliteration of the Tao Te Ching, completed just a few years ago, an astonishing discovery was revealed. The actual syntax used in this ancient text sounds strikingly familiar to modern ears. The passages sound as if they could have been written by Master Yoda.

Now, we all know that Star Wars is just a myth, written by George Lucas, late in the 20th century. Yet, we also know that most myths are, in fact, usually based upon real people and events, from long ago. Is it possible that George Lucas was a fan of ancient Taoist literature, and that he based the character of Yoda on Lao Tzu? Likewise, he could have based the idea of a mysterious and all-powerful 'Force' upon the teachings in the Tao Te Ching about the all-powerful Tao. But even if he didn't, there is still something of a mystery here.

The mystery is that in all previous English translations available, the writing of the Tao Te Ching sounded nothing like that of Yoda. Rather, English translators labored to create flowery and elegant poetry thought to reflect the eloquence of Lao Tzu. They were nothing like the foreign sounding, broken English syntax of Yoda. It was not until this new translation was completed just a few years ago, that the actual voice of Lao Tzu was heard for the first time in English. So, how could George Lucas have possibly known how Lao Tzu spoke 2600 years ago?

Lucas couldn't possibly have known this 35 years ago. There was no translation like this available at that time. Yet, this now famous Yoda-speak style of syntax and phrasing is very much how the lines of Lao Tzu read in the most recent translation. Ironically, it is not only the style of the text, but the philosophy too that is amazingly similar to the Tao Te Ching, in ways that Lucas could not possibly have known at the time.

An example of this uncanny connection between the philosophy of Lao Tzu and that of Star Wars can be found in the title Tao Te Ching. We know that Tao means Way or Path. We know that Te means Virtue, and Ching means Book or Passages. So, Tao Te Ching means approximately a Book on the Virtues of the Way, in Chinese. At least, that is what we all thought. But, what most people didn't know until recently is that the oldest version of the Tao Te Ching had the characters reversed, so it reads Te Tao Ching, which means more like The Way of Virtue.

In Chinese, Te means literally an upright heart in action. This often is thought of as goodness, but there's another meaning. An older and less well-known definition of virtue means an effective force, a potency or a power, as in *"this medicine has the virtue of reducing fevers."* Now here's the really weird part. When you take this ancient and not well known definition of virtue meaning "force" and plug it into what we now know is the original title of the Tao Te Ching, the meaning in English becomes 'The Way of the Force'. And, George Lucas had no way of knowing this back in the 1970's when he wrote it. No one did.

How can we explain this? We cannot, but it did get some of us to thinking. We decided to try a little experiment. We wanted to see what would happen if we took this most recent translation of the Tao Te Ching, and embellished it a bit. According to the above analysis, we now know that wherever the text says Tao, or the Way, it really means the Way of the Force. So, we wanted to see what would happen if we substituted the words the 'Force' or the 'Way of the Force' everywhere the Chinese character Tao appears. Then everywhere it says 'holy man' we put 'Jedi'.

The result was simply astonishing. It was a perfect fit. All 81 passages sounded as if they were undiscovered pearls of wisdom from our most beloved of pop icons, Master Yoda. If you loved the philosophy of The Force in Star Wars, and wanted more, this is it. Best of all, it's real. This was not created by a writer from our century, nor even from the last millennium. This really is one of the oldest books in the world, written many centuries before Christ. Some speculate that these verses could be even older than we think. These verses, many of them rhyming with a distinctive cadence, could have been passed down through oral tradition for centuries or even millennia, before finally being written down 2600 years ago, once a written language had been developed to do so. If that is the case, then these verses could date back to the late Neolithic Age, making them among the oldest known writing in the world.

For more information on the history and philosophy of the Tao Te Ching, look for The Secret Tao, by D. W. Kreger, which contains an archaeological and historical analysis of the origin and meaning of Taoism, along with the original transliteration that this book is based upon, and a modern English interpretation of the verses.

BOOK 1: TAO

THE WAY OF THE FORCE

PASSAGE 1

FORCES CAN BE FORCED
NOT THE ETERNAL FORCE

NAMES CAN BE NAMED
NOT THE ETERNAL NAME

UN-NAMED, HEAVEN AND EARTH IT BEGOT
BEING NAMED, OF ALL THINGS IT IS MOTHER

THUS, ONE'S NATURE NOT BEING DESIRE
IT'S SEEING HER WONDERS

ONE'S NATURE BEING DESIRE
IT'S SEEING HER ILLUSIONS

COMPARE THESE TO EACH OTHER
TOGETHER THEY ARISE, BUT DIFFER IN NAME

TOGETHER CALL THEM MYSTERIES
MYSTERY OF MYSTERIES

TO ALL WONDERS, A DOORWAY

PASSAGE 2

THROUGHOUT THE GALAXY,
IT IS KNOWN THAT BEAUTY ACTING BEAUTIFUL
REVEALS UGLY SIDE
IT IS KNOWN THAT GOOD ACTING GOOD
REVEALS NOT GOOD SIDE

THUS, BEING AND NON-BEING MUTUALLY EXIST
DIFFICULT AND EASY, MUTUALLY EXPERIENCE
LONG AND SHORT, MUTUALLY CONTRAST
TOP AND BOTTOM, MUTUALLY POSITION
VOICE AND SOUND, MUTUALLY SYNCHRONIZE
BEFORE AND AFTER, MUTUALLY SEQUENCE

THEREFORE IT IS, A JEDI
EMPLOYS NON-ACTION TO CONTEND
PRACTICE, NOT WORDS, HAVE THEY TO TEACH

TEN THOUSAND THINGS COME AND GO, YET NOT DISRUPT
GIVE-BIRTH, YET NOT POSSESS
ACT, YET NOT EXPECT
WORK ACCOMPLISHED, YET PROFIT UNCLAIMED

A WORKER ONLY WITH THEIR PROFIT UNCLAIMED
THEREFORE IS SUSTAINABLE

PASSAGE 3

NOT PRAISING ACCOMPLISHMENTS
CAUSES PEOPLE TO NOT COMPETE

NOT VALUING THE COLLECTION OF PRECIOUS THINGS
CAUSES PEOPLE TO NOT STEAL

NOT SEEING WHAT CAN BE DESIRED
CAUSES PEOPLE'S HEARTS NO CONFUSION

THEREFORE IT IS THE JEDI'S ORDER
EMPTY THEIR MIND, FILL THEIR BELLY
SOFTEN THEIR AMBITION, HARDEN THEIR BONES

THE ETERNAL NATURE MOTIVATING PEOPLE,
NOT BEING KNOWLEDGE,
NOT BEING DESIRE,
FOLLOWERS OF THE DARK SIDE, NOT DO THEY DARE ACT

ENACT NON-ACTION
THEN NOTHING IS NOT IN ORDER

PASSAGE 4

THE FORCE IS EMPTY LIKE A VESSEL
AND WHETHER USED, NOT FULL

SO DEEP IS IT
OF ALL THINGS, IT IS ANCESTOR

BLUNTS OUR SHARPNESS, IT DOES
UNTIES OUR KNOTS
SOFTENS OUR GLARE
AND MAKES US ONE WITH THE EARTH

HIDDEN DEEP
IT EXISTS FROM WITHIN
I DO NOT KNOW
OF WHO OR WHAT IT IS THE CHILD

OUR EMPERORS, IT PRECEDED

PASSAGE 5

HEAVEN AND EARTH, NOT MERCIFUL
ITS TEN THOUSAND THINGS TREATED AS STRAW DOGS

THE JEDI, NOT MERCIFUL
THEIR FOLLOWERS TREATED AS STRAW DOGS

HEAVEN AND EARTH
PERCEIVE ITS SPACE, BEING THAT OF A BELLOWS
EMPTY, YET NOT WITHOUT POTENTIAL
WHEN IT MOVES, MORE COMES OUT

ANY MORE WORDS, LESS SIGNIFICANT, NOT GOOD
STAY CENTERED, FEEL THE FORCE

PASSAGE 6

VALLEY SPIRIT NOT DYING
IS CALLED THE MYSTERIOUS ANIMA

MYSTERIOUS ANIMA, A DOORWAY IT IS
IS CALLED HEAVEN AND EARTH'S ROOT-SOURCE

FAINT, FAINT, AS IF A SOMETHING IN THE AIR
YET USE OF IT, NOT LIMITED

PASSAGE 7

HEAVEN EVERLASTING
EARTH PERPETUAL

HEAVEN AND EARTH,
EVERLASTING AND PERPETUAL ARE THEY
BY THEIR SELFLESS LIVING
THUS, HAVE THEY EVERLASTING LIFE

THEREFORE IT IS, THE JEDI
BEHIND IS THEIR PLACE, YET PLACE ABOVE
OUTSIDE IS THEIR PLACE, YET PLACED WITHIN

IS IT NOT BY BEING SELFLESS
THUS, IS ONE ABLE TO FULFILL THEIR SELF?

PASSAGE 8

HIGHEST GOOD IS LIKE WATER
WATER GIVES LIFE TO TEN THOUSAND THINGS,
BUT NOT DOES IT COMPETE

CONDUCTS ITSELF TO LOWLY PLACES, PEOPLE CONSIDER UGLY
THUS IT APPROXIMATES THE FORCE

DWELL, GOOD LAND
MIND, GOOD DEPTH
RELATE, GOOD PERSON
SPEAK, GOOD TRUTH
GOVERN, GOOD JUDGMENT
WORK, GOOD COMPETENCE
ACT, GOOD TIMING

ONE DOES NOT COMPETE
THUS, DOES ONE NOT TEMPT THE DARK SIDE

PASSAGE 9

TO GRASP BUT MORE THAN ENOUGH
NOT DOES IT BENEFIT ONESELF

A WOODEN BLADE OVER-SHARPENED
NOT CAN IT LAST LONG

JADE AND GOLD OF THE FINEST
NOTHING IS ABLE TO GUARD

WEALTHY AND HONORED ONE BECOMES
SELF-IMPORTANCE THEIR DOWNFALL

WORK COMPLETED
REMOVE YOURSELF
HEAVEN'S WAY

PASSAGE 10

BLOOD AND BREATH EMBRACING TO BECOME ONE
ABLE WITHOUT SEPARATION, EH?

CONCENTRATE QI FOR RESILIENCY
ABLE TO BECOME A NEWBORN, EH?

FOCUS AND CLEAN THE DARK MIRROR
ABLE WITHOUT IMPERFECTION, EH?

LOVE PEOPLE AND BRING ORDER TO THE NATION
ABLE WITHOUT KNOWLEDGE, EH?

HEAVEN'S GATE OPENS AND CLOSES
ABLE WITHOUT THE FEMALE, EH?

BRIGHT WHITE TO THE FOUR REACHES
ABLE WITHOUT ACTION, EH?

CREATE, AND NURTURE WHAT YOU CREATE
CREATE, BUT NOT POSSESS
ACT BUT NOT EXPECT
GROW STRONG BUT NOT DOMINATE

IS CALLED THE MYSTERIOUS VIRTUE

PASSAGE 11

THIRTY SPOKES CONVERGE TO A SINGLE HUB
NOTE IT'S THE NON-BEING OF HUB THAT IS USEFUL

SHAPE CLAY TO MAKE A POT
NOTE IT'S THE NON-BEING OF POT THAT IS USEFUL

CUT DOORS AND WINDOWS TO MAKE A HOUSE
NOTE IT'S THE NON-BEING OF HOUSE THAT IS USEFUL

THUS,
BEING, ITS ACTION, POTENTIAL
NON-BEING, ITS ACTION, USEFUL

PASSAGE 12

TOO MANY SIGHTS DRIVE A PERSON'S EYES BLIND
TOO MANY SOUNDS DRIVE A PERSON'S EARS DEAF
TOO MANY FLAVORS DRIVE A PERSON'S MOUTH TASTELESS

RACING AROUND, SEEKING ADVENTURE,
DRIVES A PERSON MAD
RARE AND PRECIOUS OBJECTS,
DRIVE A PERSON TO DO WRONG

THEREFORE IT IS, A JEDI
ACTS FROM THE GUTS, NOT ACTS FROM THE EYES
THUS, LETS GO OF ONE AND CHOOSES THE OTHER

PASSAGE 13

GLORY OR SHAME, WHICH EVER HAPPENS, IS SHOCKING
RANK GREAT DISASTERS AS IF PERSONAL

WHAT DOES IT MEAN:
GLORY OR SHAME, WHICHEVER HAPPENS, IS SHOCKING?

GLORY, WHEN IT HAPPENS, IS A SHOCK
WHEN YOU LOSE IT, ALSO IS IT A SHOCK
IS CALLED:
"GLORY OR SHAME, WHICHEVER HAPPENS, S SHOCKING"

WHAT DOES IT MEAN:
RANK GREAT SUFFERING AS IF PERSONAL?

I, HAVING HEARD REPORTS OF GREAT SUFFERING,
ACT, DO I, IT BEING PERSONAL
CONTACT WITH ME, NOT BEING PERSONAL,
WHAT SUFFERING HAVE I?

THUS IS IT,
RANKING, ITS PERSONAL ACTION THROUGHOUT THE WORLD
IT FOLLOWS, CAN BE ENTRUSTED WITH THE WORLD

LOVING, ITS PERSONAL ACTION THROUGHOUT THE WORLD
IT FOLLOWS, CAN BE TRUSTEE OF THE WORLD

PASSAGE 14

LOOK OF IT, NOT SEEN, CALL IT 'NOTHING THERE'
SOUND OF IT, NOT HEARD, CALL IT 'VERY RARE'
GRASP OF IT, NOT TOUCHED, CALL IT 'THINNER THAN AIR'

CONSIDER THESE THREE PHRASES,
NOT CAN THEY BE UNDERSTOOD
THUS, COMBINE THEM AND MAKE ONE

ITS TOP, NOT REFLECTING LIGHT
ITS BOTTOM, NOT DARKENED

EVOLVING, EVOLVING, NOT CAN IT BE NAMED
UNTIL RETURNING TO NOTHINGNESS

IS ACTING AS A NON-IMAGE IMAGE
NOTHINGNESS, ITS FORM
IS SAID TO BE 'LIKE A SHADOW'

CONFRONT IT, NOT SEE ITS BEGINNING
FOLLOW IT, NOT SEE ITS END

KEEP TO THE ANCIENT FORCE
CONTROL OF THE PRESENT, IT HAS

KNOWING THE ANCIENT PRECEPTS
IS CALLED THE WAY OF THE FORCE

PASSAGE 15

IN ANCIENT TIMES, HIGHEST-GOOD ACTED THE JEDI

SUBTLE, WONDROUS, MYSTERIOUS, AND OPEN
THEIR DEPTH, NOT CAN IT BE FATHOMED

BECAUSE NOT CAN THEY BE FATHOMED
THUS ARE THEY DESCRIBED

CAREFUL, AS CROSSING A RIVER IN WINTER
ALERT, AS ONE EXPECTING DANGER FROM ALL SIDES
DIGNIFIED, AS A GUEST
YIELDING, AS MELTING SNOW
PURE, AS UN-CARVED BLOCK
EMPTY, AS A VALLEY
MIXED, AS MUDDY WATER

WHO IS ABLE TO SETTLE MUDDY WATER,
MAKING IT CLEAR? EH?
WHO IS ABLE TO BE STILL SO LONG,
THEY CAN ANIMATE LIFE? EH?

THOSE WHO CONSIDER THE FORCE
DO NOT DESIRE TO BE FULL
ONLY ONE NOT FULL
THUS IS ABLE TO BE SUSTAINABLE

PASSAGE 16

BE COMPLETELY EMPTY
MAINTAIN TRANQUILITY

TEN THOUSAND THINGS
ARISE AND FALL

I OBSERVE THEIR CYCLE
THINGS MATURE, MULTIPLY, MULTIPLY,
AND RETURN TO THEIR ROOT

RETURNING TO THE ROOT, IS TRANQUILITY
IS CALLED THE CYCLE OF DESTINY

THE CYCLE OF DESTINY IS OUR ETERNAL NATURE
TO KNOW OUR ETERNAL NATURE IS ENLIGHTENMENT
TO NOT KNOW OUR ETERNAL NATURE IS DISASTER

KNOWING OUR ETERNAL NATURE, ONE IS ACCEPTING
ACCEPTING, THEN MERCIFUL
MERCIFUL, THEN NOBLE
NOBLE, THEN HEAVENLY
HEAVENLY, THEN WITH THE FORCE
WITH THE FORCE, THEN SUSTAINABLE

DEATH OF THE BODY IS NOT EXTINCTION

PASSAGE 17

THE MORE SUPERIOR ONE IS, THE LESS OPINIONS HAVE THEY

ONE INFERIOR PASSIONATELY ADVOCATES
ONE INFERIOR FEARS
ONE INFERIOR INSULTS
FAITH NOT IS ENOUGH, FOR ONE WITH NOT ENOUGH FAITH

TAKE TIME, HOW ONE VALUES WORDS
WHEN EVENTS HAVE TRANSPIRED
PEOPLE ALL SAY "NATURALLY! OF COURSE! CORRECT!"

PASSAGE 18

THE GREAT FORCE IS BECOMING LOST,
BEING HUMANISM AND JUSTICE FOUND

INTELLIGENCE AND CLEVERNESS APPEAR
BEING HYPOCRISY AT WORK

FAMILY NOT IN ORDER
BEING DEVOTION EXPRESSED

NATIONS FALLS INTO CHAOS
BEING PATRIOTIC MINISTERS PRESENT

THE TAO OF YODA

PASSAGE 19

DIVORCE HOLINESS AND RENOUNCE INTELLIGENCE
AND PEOPLE BENEFIT ONE HUNDRED FOLD

DIVORCE HUMANISM AND RENOUNCE JUSTICE
AND FAMILY AFFECTION RETURNS

DIVORCE SHREWDNESS AND RENOUNCE PROFIT
AND THIEVERY IS UNKNOWN

CONSIDER THESE THREE STATEMENTS
ITS ACTION FALSE, NOT SUFFICIENT
THUS, A JEDI NEED ONLY KNOW THIS

SEE THE SIMPLICITY
BECOME UN-CARVED BLOCK
FORGET THE SELF
TAME DESIRE

24

PASSAGE 20

GIVE UP STUDY, NOT HAVING PROBLEMS TO SOLVE
BETWEEN YES AND NO, WHAT IS THE DIFFERENCE?
BETWEEN GOOD AND EVIL, WHAT IS THE DISTANCE?
A PERSON WHO HAS FEAR, NOT CAN NOT FEAR

THEIR DEEP WANTING, LEADS FURTHER WITHOUT LIMIT
EVERYONE IS MERRY MERRY,
AS IF FEASTING ON A SACRIFICIAL OX
AS IF SITTING ON A TERRACE IN SPRING

I ALONE AM EXPRESSIONLESS
AS A CHILD BEFORE IT SMILES
WANDERING, WANDERING
AS IF ONE WITHOUT A HOME

EVERYONE HAS SO MUCH
BUT I ALONE SEEM TO HAVE LOST MY POSSESSIONS
MINE IS A FOOL'S MIND
INNOCENT, INNOCENT

COMMON PERSON, BRIGHT BRIGHT
I ALONE AM DIM DIM
COMMON PERSON, SHARP SHARP
I ALONE AM DULL DULL

AIMLESS AS THE OCEAN
BOUNDLESS AS THE WIND
EVERYONE HAS A ROLE IN SOCIETY
BUT I ALONE AM IGNORANT AND UNCIVILIZED

I ALONE DIFFER FROM OTHERS
AND VALUE THE SUSTENANCE OF THE MOTHER

PASSAGE 21

CULTIVATED VIRTUE FOUND
THE FORCE FOLLOWED

THE FORCE BEHAVES LIKE SO
ELUSIVE, ALWAYS DISAPPEARING, IT IS

ALWAYS DISAPPEARING, ELUSIVE
ITS CORE BEING A PATTERN, IT IS

ELUSIVE, ALWAYS DISAPPEARING
ITS CORE CONTAINING SOMETHING, IT DOES

DIM AND DARK
ITS CORE BEING AN ESSENCE, IT IS

ITS ESSENCE, REALITY
ITS CORE BEING TRUTH, IT IS

FROM BEGINNING TO PRESENT, ITS NAME NOT LOST
EVIDENT IN THE CREATION OF THE UNIVERSE, IT IS

HOW DO I KNOW OF THE CREATION OF THE UNIVERSE?
THIS IS IT!

PASSAGE 22

YIELD, BECOME WHOLE
BEND, BECOME STRAIGHT

EMPTY YOUR MIND, BECOME FULL
EXHAUST YOURSELF, BECOME RENEWED

HAVE LITTLE, BECOME ENRICHED
HAVE MUCH, BECOME PREOCCUPIED

THEREFORE IT IS, A JEDI
EMBRACES THE ONENESS
ACTING, THROUGHOUT THE GALAXY, AS A GUIDE

NOT SELF-LOOKING
THUS INSIGHTFUL

NOT SELF-STATING
THUS MAKING A STATEMENT

NOT SELF-ADVERTISING
THUS BEING NOTICED

NOT SELF-PROMOTING
THUS ADVANCING

BECAUSE THEY DO NOT CONTEND
THUS, IN ALL THE GALAXY,
NOTHING IS ABLE TO CONTEND WITH THEM

ANCIENT THE WORDS: YIELD, BECOME WHOLE
CONSIDER THIS FALSE VERSE?

BE SINCERELY WHOLE
AND TO YOU, IT WILL COME!

PASSAGE 23

NATURE'S WAY EXPRESSES ITSELF IN WHISPERS
THUS GALE WINDS NOT LAST A MORNING
THUNDERSTORMS NOT LAST A DAY

WHAT MAKES THIS SO?
HEAVEN AND EARTH, THEY ARE UNABLE TO ENDURE LONG
HOW MUCH MORE CAN DO A HUMAN?

THUS, ONE WHO FOLLOWS DEVOUTLY, AND THE FORCE
TOGETHER, BRINGS THE WAY OF THE FORCE
TOGETHER, BRINGS VIRTUE
TOGETHER, BRINGS LOSS

TOGETHER, BRINGS VIRTUE
THE FORCE DOES BRING VIRTUE

TOGETHER, BRINGS LOSS
THE FORCE ALSO BRINGS LOSS

PASSAGE 24

STAND ON TIPTOES, STEADY ONE IS NOT
WALK IN GREAT STRIDES, KEEP GOING ONE CANNOT

SELF LOOKING, INSIGHT ONE HAS NOT
SELF STATING, A STATEMENT ONE MAKES NOT
SELF ADVERTISING, NOTICED ONE IS NOT
SELF PROMOTING, ADVANCED ONE IS NOT

BEING WITH THE FORCE
THESE ARE DAY-OLD FOOD,
CARRYING EXCESS BAGGAGE,
THINGS, THE RESOURCES OF EVIL, ARE THEY

THUS BEING WITH THE FORCE, ONE EMBRACES THEM NOT

PASSAGE 25

BEING SOMETHING MYSTERIOUS AND CHAOTIC
EXISTING BEFORE HEAVEN AND EARTH WERE BORN
SILENT
EMPTY
SINGULAR, UNIQUE
ETERNAL
SPIRALING OUT, UNFOLDING AND UNENDING
COULD BE, ITS ACTION IS THE MOTHER OF CREATION

I DO NOT KNOW ITS NAME
FORCED TO CHARACTERIZE IT, IT IS SAID TO BE THE FORCE
FORCED TO NAME IT, IT IS SAID TO BE GREAT
GREAT, IT IS SAID TO BE FLOWING OUTWARD
FLOWING OUTWARD, IT IS SAID TO BE INFINITE
INFINITE, IT IS SAID TO BE RETURNING UNTO ITSELF

THUS THE FORCE IS GREAT
HEAVEN IS GREAT
EARTH IS GREAT
HUMANS, ALSO GREAT

THE WORLD, AT ITS CORE, HAVING FOUR GREAT DIMENSIONS
AND HUMANS, CLAIM THEIRS AS ONE

HUMANS EVOLVED FROM EARTH
EARTH EVOLVED FROM HEAVEN
HEAVEN EVOLVED FROM THE FORCE
THE FORCE EVOLVED AS NATURE

PASSAGE 26

HEAVY ACTS AS THE ROOT OF LIGHT
AS TRANQUILITY ACTS AS THE MASTER OF IMPULSE

THEREFORE IT IS, A JEDI,
ALL DAY THEY TRAVEL
NOT MISPLACING THEIR HEAVY LOAD

THOUGH BEING AMONG GREAT WALLS AND TOWERS
THEY FIND PEACE IN NATURE

HOW IS IT, OF TEN THOUSAND SHIPS, ONE IS LORD
YET THEIR POSITION, TAKEN LIGHTLY IN THE GALAXY?

LIGHT STANDARDS, LOSE THE ROOT
IMPULSIVE STANDARDS, LOSE CONTROL

PASSAGE 27

BEST TRAVEL, NOT LEAVING TRACKS
BEST WORDS, NOT STUTTERED
BEST CALCULATION, NOT USING SCRATCH PAPER
BEST DOOR CLOSURE, NOT BOLTED YET CANNOT BE OPENED
BEST BINDING, NOT TIED WITH ROPE YET CANNOT BE UNTIED

THEREFORE IT IS, A JEDI
ETERNAL NATURE TO BE BEST AT SALVAGING PEOPLE
THUS, THROWS AWAY NO ONE
ETERNAL NATURE TO BE BEST AT SALVAGING THINGS
THUS, THROWS AWAY NOTHING
IS CALLED ACTING FROM INSIGHT

THUS, THE BEST PEOPLE ARE, FOR THE NOT GOOD, EXAMPLES
AND THE NOT GOOD ARE, FOR THE BEST PEOPLE, POTENTIAL

TO NOT VALUE THE EXAMPLE
TO NOT LOVE THE POTENTIAL
THOUGH MAYBE CLEVER, IS GREAT CONFUSION

IS CALLED ESSENCE OF WONDERS

PASSAGE 28

KNOW THE MALE, KEEP TO THE FEMALE
ACTING AS EARTH'S LITTLE VALLEY

ACTING AS EARTH'S LITTLE VALLEY
ETERNAL NATURE OF VIRTUE NOT DEVIATING

ETERNAL NATURE OF VIRTUE NOT DEVIATING
RETURN TO ORIGINAL, AS YOU WERE BORN

KNOW GLORY, KEEP TO HUMILITY
ACTING AS EARTH'S VALLEY

ACTING AS EARTH'S VALLEY
ETERNAL NATURE OF VIRTUE NOT CORRUPTED

ETERNAL NATURE OF VIRTUE NOT CORRUPTED
RETURN TO ORIGINAL, UN-CARVED BLOCK

KNOW THE WHITE, KEEP TO THE BLACK
ACTING AS EARTH'S GUIDE

ACTING AS THE EARTH'S GUIDE
ETERNAL NATURE OF VIRTUE NOT WAVERING

ETERNAL NATURE OF VIRTUE NOT WAVERING
RETURN TO ORIGINAL, NOT BEING POLARIZED

THE UN-CARVED BLOCK, ONCE CUT, MAKES PAWNS
A JEDI'S USE OF IT, THE CUT MAKES LEADERS
THUS GREAT CARVING DOES NOT CUT AWAY

PASSAGE 29

THOSE WHO SEEK TO IMPROVE THE EARTH AND FORCE IT
I SEE THEM NOT SUCCEEDING FOR THEMSELVES

THE EARTH IS A SPIRITUAL VESSEL,
NOT CAN IT BE TAMPERED WITH

IF ONE TRIES TO CONTROL IT
ONE LOSES IT

THUS, THINGS SOMETIME LEAD, SOMETIME FOLLOW
SOMETIME BREATH HARD, SOMETIME GO EASY
SOMETIME GROW POWERFUL, SOMETIME WEAKEN
SOMETIME RISE, SOMETIME FALL

THEREFORE IT IS, A JEDI
FORFEITS ANY MORE THAN WHAT IS NECESSARY
FORFEITS ANY BETTER THAN WHAT IS NATURAL
FORFEITS ANY FASTER THAN WHAT COMES IN TIME

PASSAGE 30

IT'S THE FORCE THAT HELPS A PERSON'S LEADERSHIP
NOT THEIR WEAPONS' FORCE IN THE WORLD
SUCH ENTERPRISE INVITES REPAYMENT

ARMY'S CAMP IN PLACE
BRUSH OF THORNS GROW

GREAT WAR'S AFTERMATH
CERTAINLY BEING DEVASTATION PRESENT

GOOD THE FRUITION, THEN STOP
NOT DARING TO TAKE MORE VIOLENT ACTION

FRUITION, BUT NOT COMPLACENT
FRUITION, BUT NOT PROUD
FRUITION, BUT NOT ARROGANT
FRUITION, BUT NOT GAINING TOO MUCH

A PROSPEROUS FRUITION, ONE'S CLAIM IS
BUT NOT DOMINATION

THINGS OF GRANDNESS AND STRENGTH,
FOLLOWED AND RESPECTED
IS CALLED 'NOT WITH THE FORCE'

THAT WHICH IS NOT WITH THE FORCE, SOON ENDS

PASSAGE 31

A LETHAL WEAPON IS A SHAMEFUL THING
ALL LIVING THINGS HATE IT

THOSE WHO KNOW THE FORCE,
WANT NOTHING TO DO WITH WEAPONS

AN HONORABLE PERSON STANDS ON THE LEFT
A BATTLE COMMANDER STANDS ON THE RIGHT

BECAUSE WEAPONS ARE SHAMEFUL THINGS
THEY ARE NOT THE TOOLS OF A JEDI
PEACE AND QUIET IS MOST PRECIOUS TO US

EVEN A VICTORY IS NOT CAUSE TO CELEBRATE
THOSE WHO CELEBRATE VICTORY,
TAKE PLEASURE IN HUMAN SLAUGHTER
THOSE WHO TAKE PLEASURE IN HUMAN SLAUGHTER,
THEIR LIFE WILL NOT BEAR FRUIT ON ANY WORLD
FOREVER WILL THEY BE HAUNTED

PASSAGE 32

THE FORCE'S ETERNAL NATURE,
NOT BEING NAMED
UN-CARVED BLOCK, DEMURE
IN ALL THE GALAXY, NOTHING IS ABLE TO OVERPOWER IT

IF RULERS, ABLE ARE THEY, TO CULTIVATE IT
TEN THOUSAND THINGS WOULD NATURALLY YIELD
BALANCE WOULD BE RESTORED TO THE FORCE
ITS SWEET, INTOXICATING RAIN WOULD FALL
PEOPLE WOULD KNOW PEACE AND ORDER
WITH NO NEED OF LAWS, RULES, AND REGULATIONS

IT BEGAN WITH THE MAKING OF NAMES
NOW THERE ARE TOO MANY NAMES
WE SHOULD NATURALLY KNOW TO STOP
KNOWING TO STOP, WE CAN AVOID DANGER

THE FORCE FLOWS THROUGHOUT THE GALAXY
LIKE A RIVER THROUGH A VALLEY
FROM BROOK TO RIVER AND BACK TO THE OCEAN

PASSAGE 33

KNOWING OTHERS, IS ONE CLEVER
SELF KNOWING, IS ONE INSIGHTFUL

CONQUER A PERSON, ONE BEING POWERFUL
SELF CONQUER, ONE BEING EMPOWERED

KNOWING SUFFICIENCY, IS ONE RICH
EMPOWERMENT PRACTICED, IS ONE HAVING WILLPOWER

NOT LOSING THEIR POSITION, IS ONE ENDURING
DYING BUT NOT DYING OUT, IS ONE SUSTAINABLE

PASSAGE 34

THE GREAT FORCE FLOWS THROUGH ALL LIVING THINGS
MANIFEST IN BOTH GOOD AND EVIL

ALL LIVING THINGS DEPEND UPON IT
AND NONE ARE EXCLUDED

USED FOR ACCOMPLISHMENTS
YET TAKES NO CREDIT

NOURISHES AND CARES FOR TEN THOUSAND THINGS
YET NOT HAS IT DESIRE TO CONTROL
ETERNAL NATURE NOT BEING DESIRE
IT CAN BE NAMED 'SMALL'

TEN THOUSAND THINGS MUST RETURN TO IT IN THE END
YET IT DOES NOT ACT AS LORD
CAN BE NAMED THE ACTION, GREAT

BY NOT MAKING ITSELF GREAT
THUS, IS IT ENABLED TO REALIZE ITS GREATNESS

PASSAGE 35

TO THOSE WHO LEARN THE GREAT WAY OF THE FORCE
ALL THE UNIVERSE COMES TO THEM

COMES TO THEM NOT HARM BUT PEACE AND ORDER
LIKE A GUEST ENJOYING MUSIC AND FOOD

THE FORCE THAT COMES FROM THE MOUTH
SEEMS BLAND, BEING WITHOUT FLAVOR

DIVINENESS OF IT, NOT SEEN
WISDOM OF IT, NOT HEARD
USE OF IT, NOT LIMITED

PASSAGE 36

TO BE WEAKENED
IS TO HAVE BEEN STRONG

TO BE SHRUNKEN
IS TO HAVE BEEN STRETCHED

TO BE KNOCKED DOWN
IS TO HAVE BEEN SET UP

IT IS SAID TO BE A WONDERFUL SECRET
THE SOFT AND FLEXIBLE
SHALL OVERCOME THE HARD AND STRONG

STRONG FISH NOT CAN ESCAPE THE YIELDING OCEAN DEPTHS
SHARP WEAPONS NOT CAN OVERSHADOW A PERSON

PASSAGE 37

THE FORCE'S ETERNAL NATURE, UN-NAMED IT IS
YET NOTHING IS NOT DONE

RULERS OF WORLDS, IF ABLE TO FOLLOW AND OBEY IT
TEN THOUSAND THINGS WOULD TAKE-ROOT AND GROW CHANGE

CHANGE, AND DESIRE APPEARING
RESTRAINED IT IS, BY ITS UN-NAMED ONENESS

EVENTUALLY THERE WOULD BE NO DESIRE
NON-DESIRE IS ITS TRANQUILITY

THE GALAXY ITSELF WOULD TAKE-ROOT AND GROW PEACE
RESTORING BALANCE TO THE FORCE

BOOK II: TE

THE POWER OF THE FORCE

PASSAGE 38

SUPERIOR VIRTUE IS NOT VIRTUOUS
THEREFORE, HAVING VIRTUOSITY

INFERIOR VIRTUE IS TRYING NOT TO LOSE VIRTUE
THEREFORE, NON-VIRTUOSITY

SUPERIOR VIRTUE IS NON-ACTION
WITH NON-BEING, ITS ACTION

SUPERIOR HUMANISM IS ACTION
WITH NON-BEING, ITS ACTION

SUPERIOR JUSTICE IS ACTION
WITH BEING, ITS ACTION

BEST RULES AND REGULATIONS ARE ACTION
WITH NO ONE RESPONDING, PEOPLE USE THEIR FISTS

THUS, LOSE THE WAY OF THE FORCE, AND VIRTUE APPEARS
LOSE VIRTUE, AND HUMANISM APPEARS
LOSE HUMANISM, AND JUSTICE APPEARS
LOSE JUSTICE, AND RULES APPEAR
RULES ARE ONLY THE SURFACE OF THE MIND'S TRUTH
AND THE BEGINNING OF CHAOS

CLAIRVOYANCE IS ONLY THE FLOWER OF THE FORCE
AND THE BEGINNING OF FOOLISHNESS

THEREFORE, GREAT PEOPLE DWELL IN DEPTH
AND NOT DWELL ON THE SURFACE,
DWELL ON THE FRUIT, AND NOT DWELL ON THE FLOWER,
THUS, REJECTS THAT, AND TAKES THE OTHER

PASSAGE 39

IN TIMES PAST, THERE WAS ONENESS

SKY OBTAINS ONENESS, IT'S CLEAR
EARTH OBTAINS ONENESS, IT'S SOUND
SPIRIT OBTAINS ONENESS, IT'S STRONG
VALLEY OBTAINS ONENESS, IT'S ABUNDANT
TEN THOUSAND THINGS OBTAIN ONENESS, THEY'RE ALIVE
NOBLES AND KINGS OBTAIN ONENESS,
THEIR ACTIONS HEAVEN BELOW ARE UPRIGHT

TAKING THIS FURTHER, ALSO WE SAY:

SKY WITHOUT CLARITY,
IS THREATENED BY POLLUTION
EARTH WITHOUT SOUNDNESS,
IS THREATENED BY EROSION
SPIRIT WITHOUT STRENGTH,
IS THREATENED BY EXHAUSTION
VALLEY WITHOUT ABUNDANCE,
IS THREATENED WITH WITHERING
TEN THOUSAND THINGS WITHOUT LIFE,
ARE THREATENED WITH EXTINCTION
NOBLES AND KINGS WITHOUT UPRIGHTNESS,
ARE THREATENED WITH DOWNFALL

HUMILITY ACTS AS THE ROOT OF HONOR
AS LOW ACTS AS THE FOUNDATION OF HIGH

RULERS OFTEN SAY THEY ARE ALONE,
UNAPPRECIATED, AND HELPLESS
CONSIDER, IS IT NOT UPON HUMILITY THEY DEPEND?
IS IT NOT SO?

THUS, THE HIGHEST RENOWN, NOT BEING RENOWN
DO NOT DESIRE POLISH POLISH LIKE JADE,
BUT SINK SINK LIKE STONE

PASSAGE 40

IN CYCLES,
THE FORCE MOVES

IN YIELDING,
THE FORCE IS USED

HEAVEN BELOW'S TEN THOUSAND THINGS,
BORN OF BEING

BEING, BORN OF NON-BEING

PASSAGE 41

SUPERIOR STUDENT LEARNS OF THE FORCE
DILIGENTLY THEY PRACTICE IT

AVERAGE STUDENT LEARNS OF THE FORCE
SOMETIMES REMEMBER, SOMETIMES FORGET

INFERIOR STUDENT LEARNS OF THE FORCE
A BIG LAUGH THEY MAKE
NOT LAUGH, NOT IS ITS ACTION THE FORCE

LIGHT OF THE FORCE,
SEEMS LIKE DARKNESS

MOVING FORWARD WITH THE FORCE,
SEEMS BACKWARDS

TRAVELING WITH THE FORCE
SEEMS LIKE BEING BOUND WITH KNOTS

GREAT VIRTUE SEEMS LIKE A VALLEY
GREAT PURITY SEEMS LIKE SOIL
TOO MANY VIRTUES SEEMS NOT ENOUGH
ORTHODOX VIRTUE SEEMS CONTRIVED
TRUE BEING SEEMS HIDDEN

BEST FRAMES ARE WITHOUT JOINTS
BEST TALENTS TAKE THE MOST TIME
BEST SOUNDS ARE THE HARDEST TO HEAR
BEST FORMS TAKE NO SPECIFIC SHAPE

THE FORCE IS CONCEALED WITHIN, UN-NAMED
IT IS PRECISELY THIS WAY THAT THE FORCE
NOURISHES AND FULFILLS ALL

PASSAGE 42

THE FORCE GAVE BIRTH TO THE ONENESS
ONENESS GAVE BIRTH TO DUALITY
DUALITY GAVE BIRTH TO TRINITY
TRINITY GAVE BIRTH TO ALL LIVING THINGS

ALL LIVING THINGS
WEARING YIN AND HOLDING YANG
THROUGHOUT FLOWS CHI
ITS ACTION, A LIFE-GIVING SYNTHESIS

PEOPLE PITY THE LONELY AND THE HELPLESS
YET THESE ARE THE NAMES OF LEADERS
THUS, ONE EITHER BENEFITS FROM LOSS
OR LOSES FROM BENEFITS

WHAT OTHERS TEACH I ALSO TEACH
ONE WHO LIVES TOO AGGRESSIVELY
DIES TOO AGGRESSIVELY
THIS PRECEPT, THE ESSENCE OF MY TEACHING

PASSAGE 43

THE WORLD'S GREATEST SOFTNESS
AS A RIDER CONTROLS A HORSE
THE WORLD'S GREATEST STRENGTH
IT WILL OVERCOME

NON-BEING
HAVING AN ENTRANCE WITHOUT OPENING
MINE, THIS KNOWLEDGE IS
NON-ACTION OF IT, HAVING BENEFIT

NO WORDS OF IT, TEACHES
NON-ACTION OF IT, BENEFITS
THE WORLD OVER, NOT MANY LEARN OF IT

PASSAGE 44

NAME OR BODY, WHICH IS OF GREATER VALUE?
BODY OR POSSESSIONS, WHICH IS WORTH MORE?
GAIN OR LOSS, WHICH IS A GREATER HARM?

THUS, EXCESSIVE ATTACHMENT SURELY HAS A GREAT COST
MANY POSSESSIONS SURELY LEADS TO LOSS

KNOWING SUFFICIENCY, NOT SIN
KNOWING STOPPING, NOT DANGER
THIS, CAN BE OUR SUSTAINABILITY

PASSAGE 45

GREAT ACCOMPLISHMENTS SEEM UNFINISHED
ITS USE, NOT ENDING

GREAT FULLNESS SEEMS LIKE INFUSION
ITS USE, NOT DRAINING OUT

GREAT STRAIGHT LINES SEEM TO BOW
GREAT CRAFTS SEEM SIMPLE
GREAT ELOQUENCE SEEMS TO TRIP ON THE TONGUE

ACTIVITY OVERCOMES COLD
STILLNESS OVERCOMES HEAT

PEACE AND STILLNESS ACTS AS THE WORLD'S STANDARD

PASSAGE 46

THROUGHOUT THE WORLD
BEING WITH THE FORCE
STRAY HORSES ARE KEPT OUT OF PLOWED FIELDS

THROUGHOUT THE WORLD
NOT BEING WITH THE FORCE
WAR HORSES TRAMPLE FIELDS OVERGROWN WITH WEEDS

NO DISASTER IS GREATER THAN NOT KNOWING
WHEN IS ENOUGH

NO CRIME IS GREATER THAN GREED

THUS KNOWING ENOUGH IS ENOUGH
IS THE NATURE OF ALWAYS HAVING ENOUGH

PASSAGE 47

NOT WALKING OUT THE DOOR
KNOW ALL THE GALAXY

NOT LOOKING OUT THE WINDOW
SEE THE WAY OF THE FORCE

THEIR WALKING MORE DISTANCE
THEIR KNOWING MORE SCARCE

THEREFORE IT IS, A JEDI
NOT MOVES, BUT KNOWS
NOT SEES, BUT NAMES
NOT ACTS, BUT ACCOMPLISHES

PASSAGE 48

WORK KNOWLEDGE,
DAILY ACCUMULATE

WORK WITH THE FORCE,
DAILY STRIP AWAY

STRIP AWAY, CONTINUE TO STRIP AWAY
ITS PURPOSE, NON-ACTION
NON-ACTION, YET NOTHING NOT DONE

TO WIN THE WORLD,
ETERNAL NATURE NOT IS IT BEING ENTERPRISING

THE EFFECT OF THOSE BEING ENTERPRISING
NOT ENOUGH IS IT, TO WIN THE WORLD

PASSAGE 49

A JEDI, NOT HAVING AN ETERNAL NATURE OF MIND
IT'S A HUNDRED FAMILIES' MIND, DO THEY MIND

THE KIND, TO THEM THEY ARE KIND
THE NOT KIND, TO THEM THEY ARE ALSO KIND
THE VIRTUE KINDNESS

THE TRUSTWORTHY, THEY DO TRUST
THE NOT TRUSTWORTHY, THEY DO ALSO TRUST
THE VIRTUE TRUST

A JEDI REMAINS PRESENT
IN THE WORLD
SHY SHY DOES ACT
IN THE WORLD
MUDDLED APPEARS THEIR MIND

A HUNDRED FAMILIES ALL PAY-ATTENTION
WITH EARS AND EYES
TO THE JEDI, THEIR CHILDREN ARE THEY

PASSAGE 50

ODDS OF LIFE, FACING DEATH
LIVE: CHANCES IN 10, BEING 3
DIE: CHANCES IN 10, BEING 3

A PERSON LIVING,
PASSING THROUGH DEATH'S PROVINCE,
ALSO IN 10, BEING 3

WHY IS IT THUS?
IT IS THE THICK SHELL OF THE FORCE

THOSE WHO LEARN OF THE LIVING FORCE,
ABROAD THEY GO,
WITHOUT ENCOUNTERING TIGER OR BUFFALO
INTO BATTLE THEY GO,
BUT NO WEAPON CAN PUNCTURE THEIR ARMOR SO

BUFFALO HORNS FIND NO PLACE TO GORE
TIGERS CLAWS FIND NO FLESH TO RIP
WEAPON POINTS FIND NO PLACE TO PIERCE THEIR ARMOR

WHY IS IT THUS?
BY THEIR NON-DEATH DOMAIN, IS IT SO

PASSAGE 51

THE WAY OF THE FORCE GIVES LIFE
THE FORCE SUCKLES IT
ENVIRONMENT SHAPES IT
LOVE COMPLETES IT

THEREFORE IT IS,
DO NOT DISRESPECT THE WAY OF THE FORCE
AND DO HONOR THE FORCE

THE WAY RESPECTED AND FORCE HONORED
NOTHING IS DEMANDED
YET ETERNALLY BY ITSELF IS GIVEN

THUS, THE WAY OF THE FORCE GIVES LIFE
THE FORCE SUCKLES IT
DEVELOPS IT
CARES FOR IT
SHELTERS IT
COMFORTS IT
NURTURES IT
AND PROTECTS IT

GIVING LIFE BUT NOT POSSESSING
DOING BUT NOT DOMINATING
NURTURING BUT NOT HARVESTING

IS CALLED THE PRIMAL FORCE

PASSAGE 52

ALL OF CREATION BEING BORN,
ITS ACTION, THE MOTHER OF CREATION

DISCOVERING THE MOTHER
IT'S KNOWING HER CHILDREN

DISCOVERING HER CHILDREN,
AGAIN, WE OBEY OUR MOTHER

BURY THE BODY, NO DANGER

CLOSE THE MOUTH
SHUT THE DOOR
DEATH OF BODY WITHOUT STRUGGLE

OPEN THE MOUTH
BUSY YOURSELF
DEATH OF BODY WITHOUT HOPE

SEE THE SMALL, BE INSIGHTFUL
OBEY THE SOFT, BE STRONG
USE YOUR WIT, BUT-AGAIN RETURN TO YOUR INSIGHT

NEVER LETTING-GO OF THE BODY BRINGS-DISASTER
THIS FOLLOWS ETERNALLY

PASSAGE 53

IF I AM BORDERING ON GOOD SENSE
I GO ON THE HIGH WAY
ONLY GIVE CAUTION

THE HIGH WAY IS WELL CLEARED
YET PEOPLE ARE FOND OF SHORT-CUTS

COURTS WELL TENDED
FIELDS WELL NEGLECTED

GRANARIES WELL EMPTY
THEIR GARMENTS GORGEOUS

THEY CARRY LETHAL WEAPONS
EAT TOO MUCH AND DRINK TOO MUCH

WEALTH AND POSSESSIONS BEING IN SURPLUS
IS CALLED INVITING THEFT

SURELY, THIS IS NOT THE WAY OF THE FORCE

PASSAGE 54

WELL GROUNDED, BE NOT UPROOTED
WELL GRASPED, BE NOT LOST
CHILDREN HONORING THEIR ANCESTORS WITHOUT END

NURTURE YOURSELF
THE FORCE BECOMES REAL

NURTURE YOUR FAMILY
THE FORCE SURROUNDS YOU

NURTURE YOUR COMMUNITY
THE FORCE SURVIVES FOR GENERATIONS

NURTURE YOUR NATION
THE FORCE BECOMES ABUNDANT

NURTURE YOUR WORLD
THE FORCE IS EVERYWHERE

THUS, YOURSELF, APPRAISE AS A PERSON
YOUR FAMILY, APPRAISE AS A FAMILY
YOUR COMMUNITY, APPRAISE AS A COMMUNITY
YOUR NATION, APPRAISE AS A NATION
YOUR WORLD, APPRAISE AS A WORLD

HOW IS IT KNOWN OF THE WORLD?
IT IS THIS!

PASSAGE 55

APPRAISE YOUR VIRTUE
COMPARED TO A NEWBORN CHILD

NEITHER SCORPION NOR SNAKE ATTACK IT
NOR TIGER MALL IT, NOR BIRD OF PREY CLUTCH IT

ITS BONES PLIABLE AND SOFT
YET ITS GRIP FIRM

NOT KNOWING OF SEXUAL UNION
YET ITS REPRODUCTIVE ORGANS, FULLY FORMED
ESSENCE OF THE EARTH

ABLE TO CRY ALL DAY WITHOUT TIRING
HARMONY OF THE EARTH

KNOWING HARMONY IS OUR ETERNAL NATURE
KNOWING OUR ETERNAL NATURE IS ENLIGHTENMENT

TO RUSH LIFE, AN AWESOME THING IT IS
MIND CONTROLLING CHI, FORCEFUL IT IS
SUCH THINGS PEAK AND DECAY
CALL IT "NOT THE WAY OF THE FORCE"

"NOT THE WAY OF THE FORCE" SOON DIES

PASSAGE 56

KNOWING, THOSE DO NOT SPEAK
SPEAKING, THOSE DO NOT KNOW

CLOSE YOUR MOUTH
SHUT YOUR DOOR
BLUNT YOUR SHARPNESS
UNTIE YOUR KNOTS
DIM YOUR LIGHT
BECOME ONE WITH THE EARTH
IS THE PRIMAL UNION

THUS,
NOT CAN ONE APPROACH
NOT CAN ONE AVOID
NOT CAN ONE HELP
NOT CAN ONE HARM
NOT CAN ONE PROGRESS
NOT CAN ONE REGRESS

THUS ACTION THE WORLD VALUES

PASSAGE 57

BY ORDER, RUN A NATION
BY DISORDER, WAGE WAR
BY NON-STRIVING, GAIN THE WORLD

HOW IS IT KNOWN THIS IS SO?
IT'S SELF-EVIDENT IN THE WORLD

MORE RULES AND REGULATIONS TO FOLLOW,
AND PEOPLE ARE POORER

PEOPLE HAVING MORE WEAPONS,
NATION IS MORE DANGEROUS

PERSON HAVING MORE TECHNOLOGY,
THINGS BECOME MORE CRAZY

MORE LAWS AND PROHIBITIONS SPECIFIED,
CRIMINALS, MORE HAVE YOU

THUS, A JEDI SAYS:
I AM NON-ACTION AND PEOPLE THRIVE
I LOVE PEACE AND PEOPLE ARE ORDERLY
I AM NON-STRIVING AND PEOPLE PROSPER
I AM NON-DESIRE AND PEOPLE ARE WHOLE

PASSAGE 58

THE GOVERNMENT CARES LITTLE LITTLE
THEIR PEOPLE SIMPLE SIMPLE

THE GOVERNMENT STRICT STRICT
THEIR PEOPLE CLEVER CLEVER

GOOD FORTUNE COMES FROM BAD EVENTS
BAD FORTUNE HIDES BENEATH GOOD EVENTS
WHO KNOWS HOW THINGS WILL TURN OUT?

THEIRS NOT BEING UPRIGHT
THE UPRIGHT WILL ACT CROOKED
THE BEST ACT BADLY
PEOPLE CONFUSED FOR A LONG TIME

THEREFORE IT IS, A JEDI
SQUARES BUT NOT CUTS
POINTS BUT NOT PIERCES
STRAIGHTFORWARD BUT NOT EXTREME
BRIGHT BUT NOT BLINDING

PASSAGE 59

TO CARE FOR PEOPLE AND SERVE HEAVEN
NOTHING COMPARES WITH ECOLOGY

ECOLOGY IS CALLED
"LEARNING HOW THINGS GROW"

LEARNING HOW THINGS GROW IS CALLED
"ACQUIRING VIRTUE"

ACQUIRING VIRTUE, NONBEING NOT OVERCOME
NONBEING NOT OVERCOME, NOTHING KNOWS ITS LIMITS
NOTHING KNOWING ITS LIMITS, COULD BE IT'S NATIONWIDE
BEING A NATION, LIKE A MOTHER IT IS
COULD BE ITS SUSTAINABILITY

IS CALLED "DEEP ROOTS WITH FIRM FOUNDATION"
SUSTAINABLE LIFE AND FARSIGHTED VISION'S WAY

PASSAGE 60

RULE A GREAT NATION AS YOU WOULD COOK A SMALL FISH

THE WAY OF THE FORCE, MANIFESTED IN THE WORLD
THE DARK SIDE HAS NO POWER
NOT THAT THE DARK SIDE HAS NO POWER
THEIR POWER DOES NO HARM
NOT JUST THAT THEIR POWER DOES NO HARM
JEDI TOO DOES NO HARM TO THEM

NEITHER THE OTHER HARMS
THUS, THE FORCE FLOWS THROUGHOUT

PASSAGE 61

A GREAT NATION IS LIKE A LOW FLOOD PLAIN
THE WORLD'S INTERCOURSE
THE WORLD'S MOTHER

THE FEMALE NATURE
BY ACCEPTANCE, OVERCOMES THE MALE
BY ACCEPTANCE, ACTS SUBORDINATE

THUS, A GREAT NATION
BY SUBORDINATING TO THE SMALL NATION
BECOMES WINNER OF THE SMALL NATION

SMALL NATION
BY SUBORDINATING TO THE GREAT NATION
BECOMES WINNER OF THE GREAT NATION

THUS, TERRITORY SUBORDINATES, AND WINS
TERRITORY SUBORDINATES, AND IS WON

A GREAT NATION DOES NOT WISH FOR MORE
THAN MANY GOOD PEOPLE TO WORK
A SMALL NATION DOES NOT WISH FOR MORE
THAN TO GET JOBS

THUS, IF EITHER POSITION IS TO RECEIVE THEIR WISH
THE GREATER POSITION SHOULD ACT SUBORDINATE

PASSAGE 62

THE WAY OF THE FORCE IS
A SANCTUARY OF TEN THOUSAND THINGS
A GOOD PERSON'S TREASURE
A NOT GOOD PERSON'S PROTECTION

FINEST WORDS CAN BE ITS HONOR
NOBLE DEEDS CAN BE ITS MAKING OF A PERSON

A PERSON WHO IS NOT GOOD,
BECOME ABANDONED ARE THEY?

THUS AT THE CROWNING OF THE EMPEROR
AND ADVANCEMENT OF THREE MINISTERS
OFFERING GIFTS OF JADE DISKS
AND A FOUR-HORSE TEAM OF STALLIONS
NOT DO THESE GIFTS COMPARE TO THE FORCE

ANCIENT, THOSE WHO VALUED THE FORCE
IS IT NOT SAID: ASK AND YOU SHALL RECEIVE?
HAVING SINNED, IT'S FORGIVENESS YOU WANT
THUS ACTION, IN ALL THE WORLD, IS VALUED

PASSAGE 63

ENACT NON-ACTION
STRIVE NON-STRIVING
SENSE THE NON-SENSORY

GREATNESS FROM THE SMALL, MANY FROM THE FEW
PAYMENT FOR HARDSHIP, ITS VIRTUE

SEE SIMPLICITY IN THE COMPLEX
IN ACHIEVEMENT OF GREATNESS, ITS SMALL DEEDS

THE WORLD'S MOST DIFFICULT WORK
EASILY CAN BE MADE SIMPLE
THE WORLD'S GREATEST WORK
EASILY CAN BE DONE IN SMALL DEEDS

THEREFORE IT IS,
JEDI STRIVES NOT TO ACT GREAT
THUS ACCOMPLISHES THEIR GREATNESS

ONE'S PROMISES, TOO EASILY GIVEN, MAKE LITTLE TRUST
MANY THINGS EASY, MADE HASTY, MAKE MANY DIFFICULTIES

THEREFORE IT IS,
JEDI CONFRONTS DIFFICULTY
THUS, IN THE END NOTHING IS DIFFICULT

PASSAGE 64

THEIR PEACE EASILY OBTAINED,
THEIR TROUBLE EASILY AVOIDED
THEIR BRITTLENESS EASILY SHATTERED
AND THEIR PIECES EASILY SCATTERED

ACTION'S TIME, BEFORE BEING
ORDER'S TIME, BEFORE CONFUSION

A TREE, BIGGER THAN CAN BE HUGGED,
IS BORN OF A TINY SHOOT
A NINE STORY TERRACE STARTS WITH A PILE OF DIRT
A THOUSAND LI JOURNEY STARTS UNDER FOOT

FORCING, SPOILS IT
GRASPING, LOOSES IT

THEREFORE IT IS, A JEDI
NON-ACTION THUS NON-FAILING
NON-GRASPING THUS NON-LOSS

WHEN PEOPLE ARE NEAR SUCCESS
TO RUSH AND FAIL, IS THEIR NATURE

WHEN, AT THE COMPLETION, JUST AS IN THE BEGINNING
NURTURING AND CAREFUL, IS ONE
THEIR ACCOMPLISHMENT WILL BE NON-FAILING

THEREFORE IT IS, A JEDI
DESIRES NOT DESIRE
VALUES NOT DIFFICULT TO OBTAIN OBJECTS
KNOWS NOT KNOWLEDGE
AVOIDS THE LOSSES OF OTHERS

HELPING TEN THOUSAND THINGS FULFILL THEIR OWN NATURE,
YET NOT DO THEY DARE USE BRUTE FORCE

PASSAGE 65

THE ANCIENTS' GOOD HANDLING OF THE FORCE
NOT TO BE EXPLOITED BY PEOPLE
PROMOTED SIMPLE-MINDEDNESS

PEOPLE'S DIFFICULTY IN BEING RULED
IT'S THAT THEIR CLEVERNESS IS MANY

THUS, IT'S CLEVER RULED NATION, NATION IS POOR
NOT CLEVER RULED NATION, NATION IS WELL

KNOW THIS, COMPARE EITHER POSITION
BOTH STEM FROM THE PATTERN'S ETERNAL NATURE

KNOWING THIS ETERNAL PATTERN IS CALLED
"THE PRIMAL FORCE"

PRIMAL FORCE REACHES DEEP AND FAR
IT CAUSES THINGS TO RETURN TO THEIR NATURE
TO THE GREAT ONENESS

PASSAGE 66

A RIVER'S MOTHER SEA,
IS RULER OF A HUNDRED VALLEYS

BY ITS GOOD SUBORDINATION
THUS CAN IT ACT AS RULER OF A HUNDRED VALLEYS

THEREFORE, DESIRE TO BE ABOVE PEOPLE
SERVES YOUR WORDS BELOW

DESIRE TO LEAD PEOPLE
SERVES YOUR WORDS BEHIND

THEREFORE IT IS, A JEDI REMAINS ABOVE
BUT PEOPLE NOT OPPRESSED

REMAINS IN FRONT
BUT PEOPLE NOT BLOCKED

THEREFORE, WORLDS WELCOMES THEM
AND NOT TIRES OF THEM

BY THEIR NOT COMPETING
THUS, IN ALL THE WORLDS
NOTHING CAN COMPETE WITH THEM

PASSAGE 67

THE WORLD REGARDS THE FORCE AS GREAT
NOT LIKE ANYTHING ELSE, IS IT

BECAUSE IT IS SO GREAT
THUS, NOT LIKE ANYTHING ELSE, IS IT

IF IT WERE LIKE ANYTHING ELSE
LONG AGO, WOULD IT HAVE DISAPPEARED

BECAUSE MINE BEING THREE TREASURES
POSSESS AND MAINTAIN THEM, I DO

ONE IS LOVE
TWO IS ECOLOGY
THREE IS NOT STRIVING TO ACT AS THE WORLD'S BEST

LOVING, THUS CAN ONE BE COURAGEOUS
ECOLOGICAL, THUS CAN ONE BE GENEROUS
NOT STRIVING TO ACT AS WORLD'S BEST,
THUS CAN ONE LEAD BY EXAMPLE

NOWADAYS
MANY REJECT LOVE BUT WANT COURAGE
REJECT ECOLOGY BUT WANT GENEROSITY
REJECT HUMILITY BUT WANT TO LEAD OTHERS

BECAUSE OF LOVE
ITS OFFENSE WINS BATTLES
ITS DEFENSE HOLDS GROUND

HEAVEN WILL NOURISH
ITS LOVE, PROTECTS

PASSAGE 68

GOOD ACTS A GENTLEMAN,
NOT AGGRESSIVE

GOOD FIGHTER,
NOT ANGRY

GOOD WINNER,
NOT COMPETING

GOOD EMPLOYER,
ACTS SUBORDINATE

IS TEACHING THE FORCE OF NOT-STRIVING
IS TEACHING MANAGEMENT OF POWER
IS TEACHING UNITY WITH HEAVEN MOST ANCIENT

PASSAGE 69

LEADERS OF ARMS HAVING SAID
I WILL NOT BE THE AGGRESSOR
EVERY ACTION, DEFENSE
NOT WILL I ADVANCE ONE INCH
BUT RETREAT A FOOT

IS TEACHING MOVEMENT THAT IS NON-MOVEMENT

DEFENSIVE PREPARATION, NON-AGGRESSIVE
DEFENSIVE STANCE, NON-ADVERSARIAL
DEFENSIVE WEAPONRY, UNARMED

NOTHING IS A GREATER CATASTROPHE
THAN TO DISRESPECT YOUR OPPONENT

DISRESPECT YOUR OPPONENT
AND YOU RISK LOSING MY TREASURES

THUS, WHEN ARMS COME AGAINST EACH OTHER
THE VICTOR WILL BE STUNG BY GRIEF

PASSAGE 70

MY WORDS EASILY UNDERSTOOD
MY DEEDS EASILY PRACTICED

HEAVEN BELOW
NO ONE UNDERSTANDS
NO ONE PRACTICES

WORDS HAVING AN ANCIENT SOURCE
DEEDS HAVING AN ANCIENT PRECEDENT

BECAUSE UNDERSTAND, THEY DO NOT
THEREFORE, UNDERSTAND ME, THEY DO NOT

KNOW ME, THEY BE FEW
RESPECT ME, THEY BE VALUED

THEREFORE IT IS, A JEDI
WEARS PLAIN CLOTHES
IN HEART, WEARS JADE

PASSAGE 71

TO KNOW NOT TO KNOW
BEST

NOT TO KNOW TO KNOW
SICK

ONE WHO'S SICK OF SICKNESS
THEREFORE IS NOT SICK

A JEDI'S NOT SICK
BY THEIR BEING SICK OF SICKNESS
THEREFORE ARE THEY NOT SICK

PASSAGE 72

PEOPLE NOT FEARING THE AWFUL
IT FOLLOWS GREAT AWFULNESS COMES TO PASS

DO NOT BE DISRESPECTFUL OF THEIR HOMES
DO NOT BE REVOLTED BY THEIR LIVELIHOOD

ONLY WORKERS THAT ARE NOT TREATED AS REVOLTING
THEREFORE DO NOT REVOLT

THEREFORE IT IS, A JEDI
SELF KNOWS, NOT SELF SHOWS
SELF RESPECTED, NOT SELF PRECIOUS
THUS REJECTS ONE AND CHOOSES THE OTHER

PASSAGE 73

COURAGE AND DARING HAVE YOU
BY KILLING OR BEING KILLED

COURAGE AND DARING HAVE YOU NOT
BY COWERING IN PEACE

EITHER OF THESE POSITIONS
WHETHER GOOD OR BAD
HEAVEN, SUCH PEOPLE, DISFAVORS
WHO KNOWS THEIR REASON?

THEREFORE IT IS, A JEDI STRUGGLES WITH THIS

THE WAY OF THE FORCE
NOT IS IT STRIVING
YET MAKES GOOD OUTCOME

NOT SPEAKS
YET MAKES GOOD RESPONSE

NOT ASKS
YET IS SATISFIED

SERENELY CALM
YET MAKES GOOD PREPARATIONS

THE WEB OF THE FORCE,
VAST, VAST, AND COARSE IS IT
YET NOTHING IS LOST

PASSAGE 74

IF PEOPLE NEVER FEAR DEATH
THEN WHY DOES DEATH THREATEN THEM?

PEOPLE'S NATURE IS TO FEAR DEATH
AND WHEN THEY ACT ILLEGALLY
WE ARREST AND EXECUTE THEM
WHO DARES MISBEHAVE?

NATURE ALONE IS IN THE ROLE OF EXECUTIONER TAKING LIFE

WORKER STRIKING WITH AXE
IN THE ROLE OF EXECUTIONER TAKING LIFE
IS CALLED
"STRIKING LIKE MASTER CARPENTER CHOPPING WOOD"

OF WORKERS
STRIKING LIKE MASTER CARPENTER CHOPPING WOOD
FEW HAVE NOT INJURED THEIR OWN LIMBS

PASSAGE 75

PEOPLE STARVING
BY THEIR LEADERS TAXING TOO MUCH
THEREFORE, STARVATION

PEOPLE DIFFICULT TO RULE
BY THEIR LEADERS BEING TOO ACTIVE
THEREFORE, DIFFICULT TO RULE

PEOPLE LIGHTLY TAKE DEATH
BY THEIR SEEKING MORE LIFE
THEREFORE, LIGHTLY TAKE DEATH

ONLY ONE NOT FORCING LIFE
IS EXAMPLE OF VALUING LIFE

PASSAGE 76

PERSON ALIVE
SOFT AND FLEXIBLE
THEIR DEATH
STIFF AND HARD

TEN THOUSAND THINGS, GREEN AND LIVING
SOFT AND TENDER ARE THEY
THEIR DEATH
WITHERED AND DRY ARE THEY

THUS, THE STIFF AND HARD
DEATH'S DISCIPLES ARE THEY
SOFT AND FLEXIBLE
LIFE'S DISCIPLES ARE THEY

THEREFORE IT IS,
ARMY HARDENED
NOT SUCCESSFUL
TREE HARDENED
GETS CUT

HARD AND GREAT
INFERIOR
SOFT AND FLEXIBLE
SUPERIOR

PASSAGE 77

THE WAY OF THE FORCE
LIKE THE DRAWING OF A BOW
HIGH POSITION, LOWERED
LOW POSITION, RAISED
BEING EXCESS, REDUCED
NOT ENOUGH, SUPPLEMENTED

THE WAY OF THE FORCE
REDUCES EXCESS
SUPPLEMENTS WHAT IS LACKING

PEOPLE'S WAY NOT IS IT SO
TAKES FROM WHAT IS NOT ENOUGH
ITS ADDITION, BEING EXCESS

WHO HAS ENOUGH
HAVING EXCESS TO SUPPLEMENT THE WORLD?
ONLY BEING WITH THE FORCE, ARE THEY

THEREFORE IT IS, A JEDI
ACTS YET NOT EXPECTS
EARNS MERIT YET CLAIMS NOT CREDIT
NOT DO THEY DESIRE TO SHOW-OFF
THEIR MASTERY OF THE FORCE

PASSAGE 78

IN ALL THE WORLDS, NOTHING IS SOFT AND FLEXIBLE AS WATER
YET ATTACKING THE HARD AND STRONG
NOTHING, IS THERE ABLE TO SURPASS IT
IT NOT BEING EASY TO DO

FLEXIBLE, IT OVERCOMES STRONG
SOFT, IT OVERCOMES HARD

IN ALL THE WORLDS,
NO ONE DOES NOT KNOW
YET NO ONE'S ABLE TO PRACTICE

THEREFORE IT IS, THE JEDI SAYS
ACCEPTING NATION'S ACTS MOST SHAMEFUL
IS SAID TO BE OF SOCIETY, A LORD
ACCEPTING A NATION'S NATURAL DISASTERS
IS ACTING AS A LORD OF THE WORLD

TRUE WORDS SEEM LIKE PARADOXES

PASSAGE 79

KNOW GREAT RESENTMENT
CERTAINLY, BEING MORE RESENTMENT
HOW CAN ITS ACTION BE GOOD?

THEREFORE IT IS, A JEDI
MINDS THEIR OWN DEBT
YET NOT DO THEY DEMAND PAYMENT OF OTHERS

HAVING THE FORCE WITH YOU,
YOU MANAGE YOUR OWN DEBT

NOT HAVING THE FORCE WITH YOU,
YOU MANAGE THE OTHER PERSON'S DEBT

THE WAY OF THE FORCE IS UNBIASED
THE ETERNAL NATURE OF A GOOD PERSON

PASSAGE 80

SMALL NATIONS, FEW PEOPLE

IMAGINE HAVING 10 TO 100 TOOLS
YET NOT USING THEM

PEOPLE RESPECTING DEATH
AND NOT TRAVELING FAR

ALTHOUGH HAVING BOATS AND TRANSPORTS
NOT BOARDING THEM

ALTHOUGH HAVING ARMOR AND WEAPONS
NOT BRANDISHING THEM

IMAGINE A PERSON CAN RETURN TO KNOTTING ROPE
AND USE IT

SWEET AND SIMPLE THE FOOD
BEAUTIFUL BUT PLAIN THE CLOTHES
COMFORTABLE AND SECURE THE HOMES
HAPPY AND DELIGHTFUL THE CUSTOMS

NEIGHBORING COMMUNITIES CAN SEE EACH OTHER
HEAR EACH OTHERS' DOGS BARKING
AND ROOSTERS CROWING
YET EACH GENERATION WILL GROW OLD AND DIE
WITHOUT DISTURBING EACH OTHER

PASSAGE 81

TRUE WORDS, NOT BEAUTIFUL
BEAUTIFUL WORDS, NOT TRUE

GOOD, THOSE NOT ARGUING
ARGUE, THOSE NOT GOOD

KNOWING, THOSE NOT RICHLY EDUCATED
RICHLY EDUCATED, THOSE NOT KNOWING

THE JEDI, NOT DO THEY HOLD ON TO THINGS
SIMPLY BY DOING,
A PERSON'S SELF-FULFILLMENT BEING
SIMPLY BY GIVING,
A PERSON'S SELF-FULFILLMENT MULTIPLIED

THE WAY OF THE FORCE
BENEFITS AND NOT HARMS

THE WAY OF THE JEDI
ACTS YET NOT STRIVES

Appendix:
Dark is Light and Light is Dark: Mystery of the Tao

This translation has been modified in several ways from the original translation of the Tao Te Ching. As was mentioned in the introduction, we have replaced the words Tao with the Way of the Force, or just the Force, and we replaced the words Holy Man with Jedi. But, there were necessarily other minor differences, that may be interesting to know.

There is one little difference that you will notice in this translation, as compared to the standard English translation by the same author. The Dark Side is quite different in the original version. That is because the issue of the dark side and the light side are very thorny issues when you seriously study the Tao. If George Lucas was basing the 'Force' on the Tao, then he got this one backwards in Star Wars. Of course, we all know that the light side is good and the dark side is bad; that is common knowledge. What is so special and unique about the Tao Te Ching is that it warns us that we may have it backwards!

Lao Tzu and the Dark Side

Lao Tzu was writing about yin and yang. Yin is the dark side, it is feminine, it is yielding and accepting, it is peace. Yang is the light side, it is masculine, it is strong, powerful, it is triumphant and rich, but it is not peace. Lao Tzu obviously felt that we had too much wealth, too much power, too much violence and unrest, and not enough peace. He refers to the proliferation of valuable possessions and lethal weapons, but says that these aspects of yang only serve to increase crime and violence, and that this is not the Tao (the Way of the Force). So, Lao Tzu says we have it backwards, he says, "Know the light, but keep to the dark."

Lao Tzu repeatedly warns us that the light side looks good, but if left unchecked it will lead to ruin. Too much of any good thing, is no good. Too much food, too much drink, too much conquest, too much action, too many valuable possessions, they look good and are seductive, but they will be our downfall. So how do we avoid our natural attraction to the yang, the light side? He says to balance the light side with the dark side. And because the light side is so seductive, we must always err on the side of the dark side.

As far as I know, George Lucas did not knowingly base Yoda on Lao Tzu, and so he couldn't be expected to reverse the polarity of standard morality. Who would ever dream of such a thing? That is exactly what is so interesting and mysterious about the original Tao Te Ching; it says something that nobody else anywhere had ever said, and it makes sense too! Too much of a good thing is a bad thing. So, we need balance. We need to have equal portions of light and dark, yin and yang. In this way, things we think of as "dark" are actually our salvation. It is the dark side that brings balance to the force in an otherwise male dominated world.

The Semanitcs of Reversed Polarity

One challenge in doing this particular translation was deciding how to deal with this curious issue of reversed polarity. If I have Yoda telling people to learn about the Dark Side, or to keep to the Dark Side, it will be confusing and upsetting to Star Wars fans, even if it might please Lao Tzu fans. So what to do?

I think the most important thing is that they are both saying the same thing, even if they have reversed wording. Think of when Yoda told Luke Skywalker that "Wars do not make one great." This is very typical of Lao Tzu. War is yang, the light side. But, yin is peace, the dark side. So there is really no significant difference between the message of Yoda and that of Lao Tzu, it is just a matter of semantics. Its like in America, a public school means a State school and not a private school. But, in Great Britain, a public school means a private school. Same words, opposite meaning. If you have two supporters of private schools, one in the US and one in Britain, they might sound like they disagree with each other, but they actually both agree.

The Final Solution

For this translation, it was finally decided to keep the same speech and polarity of Yoda, even if it appears to be opposite of Lao Tzu. After all, the point of this book is to show you the Tao Te Ching, as told by Master Yoda. And this necessarily led to many changes from the standard English translation.

First, everywhere it says "dark", meaning the dark side (yin), we translated it as "mysterious". This is the figurative meaning of the word dark in Chinese, and most standard translations of Lao Tzu use this word anyway. This works well since the Force, in general, is very mysterious. Second, anytime a bad person or a bad force is referred to in the verses it is usually referred to as the "the dark side", or "those who follow the dark side." Lastly, while direct reference to light vs. dark, are changed, the other references to light vs. heavy or white vs. black (which are actually part of the same yin:yang dichotomy) are kept in their original form, to preserve consistency with the original.

All of these changes resulted in a different text indeed than the original standard translation. But, now you know that, as different as it looks, the meaning really is precisely the same, it has only been translated into Yoda's world. The message remains astonishingly similar.

About the Author

D. W. Kreger

Dr. Kreger is a psychologist, an expert on the occult, and a researcher in the fields of psychology, archaeology, and ancient mysticism. He holds a Ph.D. in clinical psychology, completed his post-doctoral training in neuro-psychology, and is a Diplomate of the International Academy of Behavioral Medicine, Counseling, and Psychotherapy. In addition to his psychological research, he has investigated archaeological sites in 17 countries around the world. His work has been presented at major academic conferences, and appeared in both research and popular media. He is the author of several books, including *The Secret Tao: Uncovering the Hidden History and Meaning of Lao Tzu*. Currently, he teaches psychology at the MacLauren Institute, and is a consulting clinical psychologist in private practice. He lives with his family on a small vineyard, north of Los Angeles, CA.

Made in the USA
Lexington, KY
02 June 2017